KATE JACKSON:

From Charlie's Angels to

Real-Life Hero

Daniel D. Johnson

1

Kate Jackson

Kate Jackson

TABLE OF CONTENTS

Kate Jackson

INTRODUCTION

Out of the glittering Hollywood world, where character depth is frequently obscured by glamor, a story that goes beyond the screen is revealed.

Welcome to "Kate Jackson: From Charlie's Angels to Real-Life Hero," an engrossing journey into the life and legacy of an actress who, more significantly than anyone, became a source of inspiration and strength outside of the entertainment industry in addition to being the famous face of Charlie's Angels.

Kate Jackson's story emerges as a narrative that transcends the realm of planned moments within the glittering Hollywood fabric. From her early years, when she was influenced by those who would later turn her into a star, to her quick ascent to fame with "Charlie's Angels," Kate's story is a tapestry of tenacity and genius.

This investigation challenges you to look past the pious exterior, past the red carpets and blazing cameras, and into the chapters that reveal Kate Jackson's actual self. We will learn about the struggles she overcame to maintain her glamorous appearance, the parts that shaped her versatility, and the acts of bravery that have made her a true force in the world.

Join us as we explore Kate's career's unexplored areas, where she played characters that had an impact that went well beyond a television screen beyond the angels.

Nevertheless, this story explores Kate's significant influence on the outside world rather than just providing a timeline of her remarkable professional life.

Kate's character emerges more clearly when we examine her charitable endeavors, her support of social concerns, and her ability to balance her personal and professional lives.

This is not just a biography; it's a monument to the resilience of a woman who turned adversities into stepping stones and emerged as a real-life hero.

Kate Jackson

So, let us go on this journey, turn the pages, and discover the numerous dimensions of Kate Jackson. Her journey from Hollywood's beloved angel to a real-life hero will inspire and strike a chord with you, demonstrating the influence that can be had off the big screen.

CHAPTER 1: WHO IS KATE JACKSON

American actress, director, and producer Kate Jackson was born in Birmingham, Alabama, on October 29, 1948. From 1976 to 1979, she portrayed Sabrina Duncan in the television series "Charlie's Angels," which brought her widespread recognition. Kate Jackson's portrayal of the astute and savvy Sabrina helped "Charlie's Angels" become a worldwide sensation.

Kate Jackson had established a successful television career before her well-known part in "Charlie's Angels," having starred in shows including "Dark Shadows" and "The Rookies."

Following "Charlie's Angels," she proceeded to exhibit her flexibility as an actor in several television shows and films. Prominent endeavors following "Angels" encompass "Scarecrow and Mrs. King" and "Baby Boom."

Kate Jackson pursued a career in directing and producing in addition to acting. In addition to producing films such as "Empty Cradle," she directed TV show episodes.

Apart from her involvement in the entertainment world, Kate Jackson has also been active in activism and charity. From being one of the first "Charlie's Angels" to having a diverse career, her trajectory demonstrates her lasting influence on the entertainment industry.

1.1 Early Years

Born on October 29, 1948, in Birmingham, Alabama, Kate Jackson had a life filled with curiosity, tenacity, and love of the arts. Born and raised in the heart of the American South, Kate's early years were influenced by a combination of her natural creative energy and Southern charm.

Her early encounters and inspirations paved the way for her to become a future star. Kate showed a strong interest in the performing arts at a young age, a passion that would eventually lead to an incredible acting career.

Her early life taught her the importance of perseverance and hard work, traits that would serve her well in her future undertakings.

Kate's involvement in the local arts scene complemented her academic pursuits while she was a student. The vibrant cultural atmosphere of Birmingham provided a fertile ground for her budding talents, setting the stage for her eventual foray into the world of entertainment.

These early years served as the foundation for the woman who would capture the hearts of audiences worldwide.

Soon, Kate Jackson would travel from the tight-knit Birmingham neighborhood to the glamorous Hollywood stages, and her formative years would prove to be the foundation for a career that went beyond the screen.

1.2 Childhood

Born on October 29, 1948, in Birmingham, Alabama, Kate Jackson spent her early years in the warm city. Her early years were influenced by the rich tapestry of a close-knit community and the soothing rhythm of Southern life, as she was raised in the heart of the South.

Being raised in a loving home, Kate's early years were influenced by the ideals of community, family, and a developing curiosity. Her love of the arts was a way for her curious nature to be shown from a young age.

From playing pretend in her backyard to taking part in school plays nearby, Kate's early activities alluded to the creative spirit that would come to define her later in life.

Although Birmingham's cultural scene provided insights into the realm of theater and storytelling, Kate's early years were also characterized by the straightforward pleasures of Southern living.

Resilience and tenacity were developed during these formative years; these qualities would be crucial for negotiating the challenging landscape of the entertainment sector.

When Kate was younger, her goals were as big as the Southern sky; they suggested that one day she would leave her village and take the stage, captivating audiences all over the world.

Kate Jackson's early adventures and formative experiences laid the groundwork for an incredible journey that would see her transform from a free-spirited Southern girl to a legendary figure in the Hollywood industry.

1.3 Upbringing

Kate Jackson was raised in an environment rich in Southern customs and family values. Kate was born in Birmingham, Alabama, on October 29, 1948, and grew up in a household that valued hard work, community, and perseverance.

Charles and Ruth Jackson, her parents, were very influential in forming the foundation of her childhood. Their advice and encouragement gave Kate a strong basis and encouraged her to follow her passions as well as a sense of responsibility.

Kate's upbringing was shaped by the diverse cultural fabric of the South, where she was raised. She developed a sense of belonging that lasted the rest of her life thanks to the close-knit community and Southern hospitality.

Kate's parents supported her artistic endeavors since they saw her early interest in the arts. Her early years cultivated the roots of a future acting career, whether she was involved in school productions or explored the local arts scene.

Integrity, tenacity, and a dedication to family values taught to her during her early years would subsequently serve as pillars in Kate's life. The woman who would become a Hollywood star and real-life hero was shaped by her background, which continued to have a strong influence even after she left the South to follow her goals.

1.4 The Family

Kate Jackson's family has played a significant role in her life, offering a strong foundation of support throughout her diverse professional career. Kate was born in Birmingham, Alabama on October 29, 1948, and her ideals and goals were greatly influenced by her family.

The supportive environment that emphasized education, hard effort, and pursuing one's passions was established by her parents, Charles and Ruth Jackson. Kate's early interest in the arts found a welcoming environment in the Jackson household, where creativity was fostered.

Even though Kate Jackson's private family life is rarely discussed, her public persona has consistently shown love and gratitude for her family.

The bonds created within the familial embrace served as a stabilizing force in the face of the constantly changing entertainment industry, despite her relocation from her Southern origins to the glitter of Hollywood.

Kate Jackson

Kate's family continued to be a pillar of support when she entered the performing world. Their support and admiration for her achievements gave her the strength to persevere and be true to her calling.

Kate's ability to manage the complexity of Hollywood while valuing the essential links that constitute family life is demonstrated by the delicate balance she strikes between a prominent career and the warmth of familial ties.

Although her career accomplishments receive most of the attention, Kate Jackson's family has had a less noticeable but no less significant impact on the story of her life, one that is fashioned by the enduring power of family bonds and is told in new chapters as they come to pass.

1.5 Influences

Kate Jackson's career and personal development have been profoundly influenced by a multitude of factors throughout her path in the entertainment industry. Kate's career was shaped by a number of things, including the supportive embrace of her Southern background and the famous performers that influenced her.

1. Roots in the South: Kate was raised in Birmingham, Alabama, and her Southern heritage imbued her childhood with traditional values, hospitality, and a sense of community. Her tenacity and sense of groundedness are partly attributed to these early influences.

2. Help from Family: Kate was given a solid foundation by her parents, Charles and Ruth Jackson, through their constant support. Their support enabled her to follow a career in the arts and explore her creative tendencies at an early age.

3. Learning Objectives: It's possible that Kate's scholastic path helped her develop her creative and intellectual skills. Her success in the entertainment sector would later be attributed to the skills she gained during her schooling.

4. The Cultural Landscape of the South: It is possible that Kate's early interest in the performing arts was sparked by the South's thriving cultural environment, which is known for its rich storytelling traditions and artistic expressions. Her artistic sensibility might have been affected by the flavours of Southern living.

5. Earlier Arts Exposure: Kate's early involvement in the arts and performance, whether through school plays or visiting neighbourhood art events, perhaps sparked her interest in acting and storytelling.

6. Emotional Signs: Famous actors who impacted Kate may have had an impact on her foray into the entertainment industry. She may have found inspiration and aspiration in the acting and actresses who came before her.

7. Difficulties Met: Obstacles on her path, whether they were personal or professional, would have surely shaped Kate's development and fortitude. Overcoming adversity

frequently moulds a person's personality and outlook on life.

The mosaic of Kate Jackson's life was built by the convergence of these various influences; it was a journey characterised by Southern charm, familial support, academic pursuits, artistic inspiration, and the capacity to overcome obstacles with grace. The actress and real-life hero that the world has come to know and love is a product of each influence.

1.6 Stepping Into the Acting World

Kate Jackson's entry into the entertainment industry signaled the beginning of a career that would extend beyond the screen and have a lasting influence. A number of crucial actions shaped her path from wannabe actress to Hollywood star.

1. Fundamental Education: Equipped with a strong academic background, Kate probably refined her abilities and acquired knowledge about the acting craft.

Kate Jackson

Her education had given her knowledge that would come in handy when she entered the cutthroat entertainment industry.

2. An early love of the arts: Kate's early love of the arts, fostered during her Birmingham upbringing, served as the impetus for her acting career. She started to display her talent and grow to love storytelling through school plays and neighbourhood productions.

3. Regional and Local Involvements: Kate may have taken use of local and regional performing opportunities before gracing the Hollywood stage. She could have developed her abilities, made contacts, and laid the foundation for a more successful career with these early experiences.

4. Debut on Television: Kate reached a major turning point when she started watching television. Her early roles in television shows like "Dark Shadows" and "The Rookies" gave her the chance to demonstrate her acting

abilities and attracted the interest of both industry insiders and viewers.

5. "Charlie's Angels" Breakthrough": The role that changed Kate's career was in "Charlie's Angels," when she played Sabrina Duncan. She became a household name and one of the top actors in the business thanks to the ground-breaking series.Her interpretation of Sabrina struck a chord with audiences all across the world by showcasing her brilliance, power, and charisma.

6. Wide Scope Moving Past "Charlie's Angels": After "Charlie's Angels," Kate's career showed remarkable flexibility. She tried her hand at several different parts in TV shows and films, one of which being a major role in "Scarecrow and Mrs King." This performance showed that she could transcend the limitations of a single well-known part.

7. Producing and Directing: Kate ventured into producing and directing in order to broaden her impact

behind the scenes. This diversification enhanced her reputation as a well-rounded artist in the entertainment industry and highlighted her many talents.

Kate Jackson's path to acting was marked by skill, perseverance, and a dedication to lifelong learning. Her rise illustrates the tenacity of a woman who not only overcame the obstacles of her field but also made a lasting impression on audiences all around the world, from the small stages of Birmingham to the glittering lights of Hollywood.

1.7 The Road to Stardom

Kate Jackson's breakthrough performance and unquestionable ascent to fame occurred when she played Sabrina Duncan in the beloved television series "Charlie's Angels." In addition to becoming a global phenomenon, this ground-breaking show launched Kate into the spotlight in Hollywood back in 1976.

Kate Jackson

1. Sabrina Duncan, the cast: Cast as one of the initial "Angels" in the series, Sabrina Duncan, marked the beginning of Kate's rise to fame. Her portrayal of Sabrina, a heroine who successfully embodied humour, charm, and strength, connected with viewers and established the foundation for the show's success.

2. Dynamic Trio: Kate created the dynamic trio of crime-fighting "Angels" with Farrah Fawcett and Jaclyn Smith. Their individual charms and on-screen chemistry combined to produce a winning formula that enthralled audiences and brought them great fame.

3. Cultural Phenomenon: "Charlie's Angels" surpassed television to become a cultural phenomenon that influenced pop culture, fashion, and how people saw women in the media. The show's extraordinary popularity was largely attributed to its distinctive fusion of action, glamour, and friendship.

4. The Legacy of Sabrina Duncan: In addition to having a profound impact on the character, Kate's portrayal of Sabrina Duncan helped "Charlie's Angels" live on forever. Sabrina's brilliance and aptitude served as a symbol of the changing expectations placed on women in television.

5. International Acknowledgment: Due to "Charlie's Angels" worldwide success, Kate Jackson gained notoriety and recognition on a global scale. She became well-known and her picture appeared on magazine covers, representing the strong, attractive women the show portrayed.

6. Routing Difficulties: Even with the show's enormous popularity, Kate had to deal with difficulties, such as disagreements over contracts, which affected her choice to leave "Charlie's Angels" after the third season. But her departure didn't lessen the influence she had on the show or television history in general.

7. Career After "Angels": Kate's exit from "Charlie's Angels" signalled a change in her professional trajectory. She demonstrated her versatility in a number of television programmes and films, demonstrating that her talent was not limited to one particular character.

Kate Jackson's ascent to fame on "Charlie's Angels" cemented her place in Hollywood history and helped define a television era. Her role in the popularity of the show is still evidence of both the cultural influence of a television series that revolutionized the medium and her acting talent.

CHAPTER 2: BEHIND THE ANGELIC FACADE

As one of the first "Charlie's Angels," Sabrina Duncan, Kate Jackson rose to fame, but the complicated and nuanced picture of her true life lies beyond the heavenly exterior. Beyond the flash and glamour of Hollywood, Kate overcame many obstacles to show a resilient and genuine lady whose path defined her.

1. Expert Difficulties: Behind the scenes on "Charlie's Angels," Kate had to deal with work-related issues like disagreements over contracts. Despite having an effect on her time on the show, these difficulties demonstrated her will to succeed in a field that is frequently characterised by complexity.

2. Leaving "Charlie's Angels": A major turning point in Kate's career was her choice to leave the show after the third season. It demonstrated her dedication to maintaining the integrity of her work as well as her wish

to play a variety of roles outside the constraints of a single, iconic character.

3. Adaptable Positions: Following "Charlie's Angels," Kate demonstrated that her talent went much beyond the glitzy realm of the Angels by accepting adaptable roles in television films and programs. This stage of her career demonstrated her range as an actor and her capacity to play a variety of roles.

4. Producing and Directing: Kate's career encompassed not only acting but also directing and producing. Her desire to participate in the creative process was demonstrated by this behind-the-scenes activity, which also strengthened her reputation as a versatile artist.

5. Activism and Philanthropy: Outside of the entertainment industry, Kate participated in activism and philanthropy, supporting groups that shared her beliefs. Her passion to having a positive impact outside of the screen was evident in her participation in philanthropic endeavours.

6. Halving Privacy and Stardom: While navigating the difficulties of celebrity, Kate showed a willingness to keep some privacy. Her genuineness and dedication to keeping some parts of herself hidden from the public were demonstrated by her careful balancing act between her personal life and celebrity.

7. Beyond "Angels" Legacy: Kate Jackson's influence is not limited to the heavenly exterior of "Charlie's Angels." Her work has had a lasting influence on the entertainment business and is a testament to her perseverance, adaptability, and commitment to her art.

Kate Jackson's real-life dynamics beneath the angelic exterior of Sabrina Duncan reveal a woman who accepted a variety of opportunities, overcame adversity with grace, and left an enduring legacy in the entertainment industry that goes well beyond the glitzy realm of "Charlie's Angels."

2.1 Behind the Scenes:

Kate Jackson's journey encompassed not just the fascinating performances in front of the camera, but also the world behind the scenes. Her forays into producing and directing demonstrated her diverse skill set and ambition to support Hollywood's artistic community.

1. Moving from Input to Output: Kate's career took a big turn when she decided to become a director. As she assumed this position, she was able to mold stories and add her artistic perspective to the projects she worked on.

2. Projects in Direction: Kate's ability to direct episodes of different television shows showcases her versatility and expertise in front of the camera. Her move from actress to director demonstrated her dedication to increasing her impact in the business.

3. Creative Projects: Kate's role as a producer further cemented her status as a formidable force behind the scenes. She made a significant contribution to project

creation as well as the realization of stories through production.

4. Creative influence: Kate had more creative influence over her work as a director and producer than she had as an actress. Her ability to impact project execution, visual aesthetics, and storytelling was made possible by this change.

5. Themes Exploration: In front of the camera, Kate experimented with many themes and storylines, demonstrating her versatility in the field. Her decisions as producer and director demonstrated a sophisticated grasp of narrative and a dedication to presenting a range of viewpoints.

6. Partnerships: Kate's willingness to work together was demonstrated by her partnerships with other business leaders. It need strong leadership, excellent communication, and the capacity to unite a group of people to realise a common creative vision to work behind the camera.

7. History of Producing and Directing: The influence of Kate Jackson goes beyond her acting roles to include her work in the background. Her continued influence on the entertainment business is demonstrated by her work as a producer and director.

Kate Jackson's forays into producing and directing gave her already remarkable career even more depth. She showed her dedication to storytelling and will to have a lasting impact on the profession from a variety of angles by accepting gigs behind the camera.

2.2 Difficulties in the Glamourous Society

Even though Kate Jackson was drawn to the bright lights of Hollywood, her path was not without difficulties. She encountered challenges navigating the entertainment industry's intricacies, which put her perseverance to the test and influenced the story of her time in Hollywood.

1. Contextual Conflicts: During her tenure on "Charlie's Angels," Kate faced contractual conflicts, bringing

attention to the difficulties that can arise when a celebrity comes with contracts. These disagreements, albeit difficult, demonstrated her resolve to make her voice heard in a field characterised by complex contracts.

2. Handling Notoriety and Seclusion: The popularity that followed "Charlie's Angels" success created difficulties in striking a balance between private and public exposure. It took a careful balance to maintain parts of her private life while juggling the pressures of notoriety.

3. From "Charlie's Angels" to Post-Transition: Releasing Sabrina Duncan from her legendary role was a significant shift. Overcoming the shadow of a cherished character and showcasing her range as an actress in a genre sometimes characterized by typecasting constituted the challenge.

4. Sector Pressures: The entertainment sector faced constant hurdles in satisfying expectations and being relevant. Hollywood's dynamic environment necessitated flexibility and fortitude in the face of changing fashions.

5. Market Environment: Actors looking for varied and important parts have difficulties in Hollywood because of its competitive environment. Kate's success in landing roles outside of "Charlie's Angels" demonstrated her resolve to overcome obstacles in the business and play a variety of characters.

6. Gender Dynamics: Actresses faced difficulties due to the historical gender dynamics in the profession, which included differences in opportunity and compensation. Throughout her trip, Kate saw how the Hollywood scene for women was changing, and she handled these changes with courage.

7. Balance between Personal and Professional: A common struggle in Hollywood is juggling busy work with a personal life. Kate's skillful handling of this fine balance was demonstrated by her ability to preserve certain parts of privacy while prospering professionally.

8. Sector Development:

Hollywood is always changing, so you have to be flexible. Kate had to navigate a constantly changing business, with technological breakthroughs and shifting storytelling trends necessitating a flexible approach to her profession.

Kate Jackson's story of her Hollywood career, filled with setbacks and victories, depicts the complex fabric of a field where obstacles and glamour coexist. Her ability to face and conquer these obstacles paved the way for a career that transcends the screen and embodies the tenacity needed to succeed in the glamorous but cutthroat world of entertainment.

2.3 Developing a Special Persona

Kate Jackson was more than just the sassy Angel dressed in sparkling clothes, Sabrina Collins. She created a distinct character behind the camera, away from the flash and glamor, that disregarded Hollywood norms and forged its own route. This is the method she used:

- From Hollywood Glamour Girl to Production Giant:

In a field dominated by men, Jackson took a risk by founding 'Mother Productions', trading in his angel wings for a producer's hat. This character was more about intelligence than beauty; it was about seizing the initiative and opening doors for other actresses. It was an image of fiery self-reliance and imaginative aspiration.

Behind the Camera, Beyond Expectations: Kate created a new persona when she took up the camera. This one was that of a director, not a helpless damsel in distress but a storyteller in charge of the narrative.

Her persona radiated quiet confidence, an unwavering focus on her vision, and a commitment to developing talent both on and off-screen. The Advocate's Edge: Kate's persona wasn't just restricted to entertainment; she also championed social causes, fighting fiercely for gender and LGBTQ+ rights with a fierceness that matched her on-screen charisma.

- Beyond Hollywood, an Intangible Legacy: Her advocacy for the environment gave rise to another aspect of her identity: the eco-warrior. She demonstrated that celebrities might be more than just pretty faces on film when she created the Environmental Media Association. This persona demonstrated a strong bond with the environment and an unwavering quest for a sustainable future.

The Key Ingredient: Genuineness Is Everything

The genuineness of Kate Jackson's persona was what made it so captivating. She had no problem sharing her challenges, being open and vulnerable, and proving that even famous people can have human weaknesses. Audiences were moved by her openness and sincere interest, which rendered her character likeable and motivating.

Lessons from the Angel Who Dare to Fly: Anyone developing their own distinct self can learn a lot from Kate Jackson's path.

Accept Evolution: Don't fit into just one category. Allow your persona to change as your values and experiences do.

- Challenge the Status Quo: Don't be scared to defy expectations and adopt a persona that goes against the grain.

Use Your Platform for Good: Make your online persona an advocate for causes you support and a force for good in the world.

Remain True to Yourself: Above all, keep in mind that the most alluring characters are those who are true to themselves.

Kate Jackson's life was more than a screenplay; it was a master class in creating a distinctive character that

Kate Jackson

impacted people's lives and went beyond celebrity. She demonstrated to us that sometimes the most compelling role you play is your own by stepping outside of the Angel wings.

CHAPTER 3: ACTING BEYOND THE ANGELS

Kate Jackson had a long career in Hollywood that went far beyond "Charlie's Angels." Her work after 'Angels' revealed a stunning creative development as she kept experimenting with different parts and adding to the fabric of narrative in films and television.

1. TV Films: Following "Charlie's Angels," Kate ventured into the world of television films, demonstrating her ability to play a variety of roles in different genres. She was able to investigate stories that extended beyond a series' episodic structure because to this shift.

2. "Mrs. King and the Scarecrow": After "Angels," Kate gained notoriety for her role in "Scarecrow and Mrs. King." Her ability to captivate viewers in a new setting

Kate Jackson

was further demonstrated by this television series, which combined elements of drama, romance, and espionage."

3. Theme Exploration: Following "Angels," Kate purposefully chose roles that addressed a range of subjects. Her characters developed into compelling storytelling vehicles, whether they were traversing the difficulties of espionage or exploring the nuances of relationships.

4. Directory Activities: By taking the helm and directing television series episodes, Kate increased her impact. Her move from performer to director demonstrated her versatility and gave her the opportunity to bring her artistic vision to the narrative process.

5. Creative Projects: Kate expanded her creative position behind the scenes by becoming a producer in addition to a director. Her production-related work demonstrated her dedication to developing characters and making stories come to life.

6. Onstage Presentations: Kate's artistic explorations went beyond the film to include theater shows. She showcased her versatility as an actress by bringing her skill to audiences in a new dimension and embracing the intimacy and immediacy of live theatre.

7. Eye Catchings: To the astonishment of her fans, Kate made brief cameos in a number of television programs. Her fleeting but significant appearances captivated spectators with flashes of her skill and confirmed her long-lasting presence in the industry.

8. The Versatility Legacy: Kate Jackson left behind a legacy of variety with her artistic development beyond "Charlie's Angels". Her career remained dynamic and ever-evolving due to her desire to embrace a variety of roles and her investigation of various aspects of the entertainment scene.

Kate Jackson's path following "Angels" is proof of her dedication to both artistic development and narrative. She never stopped captivating audiences whether in front of the camera, behind the scenes, or on stage, making a lasting impression on the changing television and film industries.

3.1 Diverse Roles and Projects Artistic Tapestry Unveiled:

Throughout her career, Kate Jackson took on a variety of roles and projects that demonstrated her versatility and dedication to narrative, creating a rich tapestry of her artistic journey. Beyond the glitzy portrayal of "Charlie's Angels," she embraced a variety of roles and endeavours that gave her extraordinary career more depth and dimension.

1. "The Rookies" and Their earliest TV roles: Prior to joining the legendary cast of "Charlie's Angels," Kate demonstrated her acting abilities in a number of television parts, including a noteworthy part in "The Rookies." Her varied career was made possible by these early encounters.

Kate Jackson

2. A Legacy of Crime-Fighting as Sabrina Duncan:
Sabrina Duncan's portrayal on "Charlie's Angels" helped
define a time period and made Kate a household name.
Her interpretation of the astute and resourceful
crime-fighter introduced a persona that came to represent
the success of the programme.

3. Television Films - An Adaptable Canvas: Following
"Angels," Kate explored a variety of genres in television
films. These roles, which ranged from gripping dramas
to moving tales, gave her the chance to demonstrate the
breadth and depth of her acting skills.

4. The Story of "Scarecrow and Mrs. King": Romance
and Espionage" Instead than focusing on fighting crime,
"Scarecrow and Mrs. King" exposed Kate to the world of
espionage and romance. She was able to showcase a
different side of her acting talent with her depiction of
Mrs. King.

5. Behind the Scenes Mastery - Producing and Directing:
Kate aggressively influenced narratives behind the

scenes as she took a chance on directing and producing. Her commitment to narrative and her desire to bring a fresh perspective to the creative process were both evident in her involvement.

6. Live Artistry - Stage Performances: Kate appreciated the intimacy and immediate nature of live performances as she stepped onto the stage. Her attempt at stage acting demonstrated her versatility as an artist and opened up new avenues of communication with viewers.

7. Delightful Surprises - Cameo Appearances: The unexpected glimpses of Kate's skill that she gave fans during her cameo appearances in numerous television shows pleased them. These fleeting but significant instances confirmed her continued influence in the field.

8. History of Versatility in Art: Kate Jackson left behind a legacy of artistic adaptability, which was molded by her readiness to take on a variety of roles and endeavors. Her varied career spanned roles such as detective and

spy, as well as live performances and television films. Her influence is felt in the entertainment industry.

Kate Jackson's varied roles and projects form an artistic tapestry that bears witness to her lasting influence in the entertainment industry. Her ability to smoothly transcend between genres and mediums validates her standing as a versatile and beloved personality in the hearts of people worldwide.

3.2 Powerful Acts

Though her most famous role was undoubtedly that of Sabrina Duncan in "Charlie's Angels," Kate Jackson's career featured a stunning diversity of roles and powerful performances that solidified her reputation as a captivating and versatile actress.

The Initial Years: Establishing Her Footing: Shadows of Darkness (1966–1971): In the Gothic soap opera "Dark Shadows," Kate made her on-screen debut as a number of characters, including Tracy Collins and Daphne Harridge.

Kate Jackson

Her ability to represent a range of personalities and work through intricate plots was refined in these roles.

The Rookies (1972–1976):

Jackson's breakthrough performance in the police drama "The Rookies" as Officer Jill Danko demonstrated her ability to handle high-stakes scenarios and give intensely felt performances.

Breaking Barriers as Sabrina Duncan: Charlie's Angels (1976–1979): Sabrina Duncan was more than simply a glamor girl in the part that launched her to global fame. Jackson gave the character humor, intelligence, and a feeling of groundedness that helped viewers relate to and find inspiration in her.

Post-Angels Explorations: Scarecrow and Mrs. King (1983–1987): Jackson demonstrated her ability to strike a mix between humor, action, and emotional depth in her role of divorced housewife-turned-spy Amanda King in this action-comedy series.

Kate Jackson

In the sitcom Baby Boom (1988–1989), Jackson portrayed J.C. Wiatt, a successful businesswoman who unintentionally becomes a mother. Her performance struck a chord with listeners as it skillfully handled the difficulties of motherhood and finding a work-life balance.

Dramatic roles and films suited for television:

In the moving television film Lover's Knot (1995), Jackson portrayed a lady fighting breast cancer with remarkable intensity. She won praise from critics for her genuineness and emotional range.

Touched by an Angel (1999): She made a memorable and profoundly emotional guest appearance as a lady dealing with a terminal illness, showcasing her ability to convey real emotion and vulnerability.

Beyond the Screen: Stage Actors: Jackson's skills were also utilised on stage, where she portrayed leading roles in popular plays such as "Love Letters" and "The Vagina Monologues."

Voice-Over: Her unique voice was used to contribute to animated series such as "The Simpsons" and "Family Guy," demonstrating her versatility as an actor.

Throughout her career, Kate Jackson has been known for her willingness to take on a variety of roles, to go against the grain, and to give each character she played depth and authenticity. Her enduring legacy as Sabrina Duncan is mostly shaped by her iconic part, but her body of work as a whole shows a tremendous diversity and a dedication to powerful storytelling.

3.3 Molding Storylines in Hollywood

The influence of Kate Jackson on the film industry goes well beyond her brilliant smile and karate kicks while playing Sabrina Collins on "Charlie's Angels." She was more than just an actress, she was a trailblazer, an advocate for social change, and a driving force behind the stories that adorned our screens. She rewrote the game as follows:

From Producer to Angel Investor:

Kate Jackson

Kate Jackson broke the mold in the male-dominated Hollywood of the 1970s. Feeling that her creative freedom was restricted on "Charlie's Angels," she founded "Mother Productions," making history as one of the first female television celebrities to produce. Many actors were able to demand more control over their careers and tales as a result of this daring action.

Beyond Entertainment: Supporting Social Issues: Jackson's impact extended beyond the small screen. She used her platform to question the current quo and become an outspoken supporter of LGBTQ+ and gender equality. She paved the way for a more inclusive industry by speaking out against discrimination and misogyny.

Transitioning from Producer to Director: Jackson didn't merely barge into the producer's office; she also took a stab at directing episodes of popular television programmes such as "Scarecrow and Mrs. King" and "Baby Boom." She demonstrated her directing prowess, adding another level of influence to her narrative shaping power, with an acute eye for detail and a flair for generating nuanced performances.

Creating a Legacy Outside of Hollywood: Kate's impact went beyond the boundaries of Hollywood.She advocated for environmental causes, use her position to spread the word about unsustainable activities and climate change. In an effort to shape a more sustainable future and use her voice for positive change, she formed the Environmental Media Association.

The Pioneering Legacy of Narrative:

The legacy of Kate Jackson is interwoven with bravery, aspiration, and an unwavering quest for equality and constructive change.Her legacy in Hollywood will never fade: She cleared the path for female filmmakers and producers.

making use of her position to promote social justice.

dispelling myths and showcasing strong, independent female characters.

encouraging sustainable behaviours and promoting environmental causes.

Proceeding with Kate's Influence: We can pay tribute to Kate's memory by:

assisting female filmmakers and creators.

calling for diversity and representation in narrative.

raising our voices in support of our convictions.

advocating for sustainable practices in the environment on a regular basis.

Not only was Kate Jackson an Angel, but she was also a revolutionary who changed the stories we saw on TV and brought about change in the real world. Her advocacy, creative aspirations, and persistent dedication to a better future serve as an inspiration to future generations.

CHAPTER 4: REAL-LIFE HEROICS UNVEILED

Even though Kate Jackson wowed viewers as the ferocious Sabrina Collins in "Charlie's Angels," her valiant deeds in real life far outweighed any thrilling television show. Beyond the glittering costumes and clever repartee, this tale unveils Kate Jackson's true self as a fearless defender, sympathetic sympathiser, and unflinching voice for justice.

- Breaking the Boundaries:

Feeling unfulfilled by Hollywood's constraints and desiring a more profound influence, Kate gave up her Angel wings and embarked on a new journey. She rose to prominence as a passionate supporter of social justice, fighting for the rights of women, LGBTQ+ people, and the environment. Her voice, magnified by her notoriety, reverberated across television and into legislative chambers, calling for equality and tearing down barriers based on discrimination.

- Overcoming Her Obstacles, Motivating Others: Kate's personal weaknesses turned into her greatest assets. By being honest about her addiction and mental health issues, she dispelled stigmas and gave others the confidence to get treatment. Her experience inspired compassion and empathy, demonstrating that true heroes don't wear masks but rather exhibit vulnerability and the bravery to face their own fears.

- Taking on Environmental Goliath: For Kate, the war for the environment wasn't a side issue. It was a campaign based on a strong bond with the natural world. She established the Environmental Media Association, a potent forum that brought together the environmental movement and Hollywood. She urged people to become stewards of our planet by challenging harmful habits, inspiring conscientious choices, and advocating through education and creative storytelling.

- A Legacy of Ordinary Heroism: Kate Jackson's bravery extended beyond overt actions. It was evident in her day-to-day behavior, her steadfast support of underrepresented groups, and her dedication to leveraging her position to effect positive change. She gave people the confidence to speak up for themselves, stand up for what they think, and create any kind of change, no matter how tiny.

- Revealing the Hero Within: Kate's tale serves as a reminder that heroes don't require magical abilities or capes. These are just regular people who have made exceptional decisions. Her example encourages us to stand up to the establishment and defend what is right.

Accept vulnerability and empower others via our struggles. Encourage initiatives we support, even when the odds appear overwhelming. Make decisions in your daily life that improve the world.

This is more than just Kate Jackson's story, it's an appeal to take charge, speak up, and change the world. And we can all decide to reach our own heroic potential, just as Kate did when she gave up her angel wings.

4.1 Magnanimous Projects

Kate Jackson was a philanthropist in addition to using her name and notoriety to support charitable causes.She actively sought to encourage positive change through a variety of activities and had strong passions for a number of causes.

Champions for Children: Children's Miracle Network: Jackson oversaw national fundraising efforts for ill and injured kids in US hospitals while serving as the organization's chairperson.

She participated in fundraising activities and spoke out in favour of St. Jude Children's Research Hospital, enthusiastically supporting the institution's life-saving efforts.

Kate Jackson

Equality & Social Justice: Jackson collaborated with the National Gay and Lesbian Task Force to fight prejudice and advance equality. Jackson was a strong supporter of LGBTQ+ rights.

Feminist Majority Foundation: She provided support for women's reproductive rights and empowerment by lending her voice to the organisation.

Environmental Champion: Environmental Media Association: Jackson was instrumental in bringing environmental issues to the attention of the entertainment industry and the general public as one of the founding members of the Environmental Media Association (EMA). She also urged famous people to promote sustainable practices using their platforms.

Earth Day Network: A fervent advocate of Earth Day, Jackson took part in activities and events meant to spark action and increase public awareness of environmental issues.

Beyond the Spotlight: Local community support: Jackson showed her dedication to changing the world wherever she lived by actively supporting a number of local charities and organisations in her areas.

Personal philanthropy: She put her convictions into reality by showing compassion and giving to others, encouraging them to return the favour in their own unique manner.

Kate Jackson's charitable legacy serves as a reminder that anybody may have a beneficial impact on the world, regardless of their level of fame or wealth. Her fervent support, hands-on involvement, and steadfast dedication to a range of social and environmental causes continue to motivate others to take initiative and build a better future for everybody.

4.2 Promoting Social Causes

Kate Jackson was a fervent supporter of social causes that went far beyond spreading awareness and endorsing initiatives. She was an outspoken supporter, a cunning

Kate Jackson

activist, and an unceasing agent of goodwill. A closer
examination into her influence is given below:

Supporting the Rights of Women:

Foundation of the Feminist Majority: Through her
participation in the Feminist Majority Foundation,
Jackson actively backed campaigns that addressed
gender-based violence, women's equality in the
workplace, and reproductive rights.

Public Voice: She advocated for legislative changes and
galvanised public support for women's interests by using
her platform to speak out against discriminatory laws
and practices.

Defending LGBTQ+ Rights: Jackson's outspoken
advocacy for LGBTQ+ rights pioneered a new chapter in
the history of prejudice. She battled against
discriminatory legislation, marched with the community,
and took part in rallies.

Fighting Discrimination: Her participation encouraged people to fight for equal rights and embrace their identities, which made society a more welcoming and inclusive place.

Protecting the ecosystem:

Association for Environmental Media: Jackson's environmental activism took a significant turn when the EMA was founded.Using her power, she brought attention to environmental issues and promoted environmentally friendly practices in Hollywood.

Beyond Awareness: She led the EMA in implementing useful programmes like the Green Seal certification programme, which forced the entertainment sector to adopt more environmentally friendly production techniques.

Strategic Activism: Forming Alliances: Jackson recognised the value of working together. She actively collaborated with other groups, well-known people, and neighbourhood movements to build her advocacy efforts and give her voice more weight.

Good Communication: She was an adept communicator, creating themes that struck a chord with a wide range of listeners and successfully galvanised support for many causes.

A Legacy of Change: Motivating Next Generations: Jackson's steadfast dedication to social justice continues to motivate activists and public figures to stand up and defend their convictions.

Concrete Impact: She became involved with groups like the Feminist Majority Foundation and the EMA, which changed attitudes, laws, and environmental practices in real ways.

4.3 Changing the World Outside of Hollywood

Kate Jackson has a reputation of changing many other fields, and her effect goes far beyond the Hollywood industry. Her dedication to issues greater than herself, whether through philanthropy or activism, shows a deep influence that goes beyond the gloss and glamour of show business.

1. Charitable endeavors: Kate was a committed philanthropist who used her platform to advocate for causes that were important to her. Her devotion to improving the lives of others was demonstrated by her charity endeavours.

2. Advocacy for Breast Cancer Awareness: Kate, who personally survived breast cancer, rose to prominence as a prominent supporter of breast cancer awareness.Her initiatives to promote research, encourage others going through similar struggles, and increase awareness had a major impact on the larger movement for women's health.

3. Environmental Advocacy: Outside of the spotlight, Kate took part in environmental advocacy and gave voice to concerns that promoted sustainable living and

conservation. Her support demonstrated a dedication to protecting the environment for coming generations.

4. Initiatives for Animal Welfare: Kate was also compassionate when it came to animal welfare, supporting programmes that tried to protect and improve the lives of animals. Her efforts demonstrated a profound sense of empathy for the voiceless people on the planet.

5. Education Promotion: Understanding the transformational potential of education, Kate backed programmes that encouraged literacy and learning. Her support of education was motivated by the desire to give people the chance to pursue their own learning and development.

6. Awareness and Education Campaigns: Kate actively participated in public awareness efforts on a range of social topics by utilizing her platform. Her participation in campaigns aimed to draw attention to important issues and promote group action for constructive change.

7. Empathies with Humanity: Kate's dedication to helping others demonstrated her desire to confront more significant social challenges. Her areas of campaigning were social justice, poverty alleviation, and assistance for marginalized populations.

8. Social Impact Legacy: Kate Jackson left behind a legacy that goes beyond the entertainment sector and has a social impact. Her commitment to changing the world inspires others to use their influence to advance societal progress.

Kate Jackson has left an enduring legacy through her advocacy work and charitable endeavors , in addition to the parts she played on television. Her legacy is proof of the transforming power that comes from using one's influence to improve the lives of others and leave a lasting impression.

CHAPTER 5: BALANCING ACT

Throughout her career, Kate Jackson showed an expert understanding of how to strike a balance between her devotion to social concerns, ambition, and personal happiness. This is how she balanced all the balls in her life:

The Early Balancing Act

Ascending Star: Kate gained enormous recognition as Sabrina Collins in "Charlie's Angels," but she never allowed it to define who she was. She showed her passion for artistic diversity by actively pursuing voice-over and theatre opportunities.

Discovering Her Voice Kate demonstrated an early dedication to using her voice for social good by using it to speak out against sexism and to campaign for gender equality, even during the height of her "Angel" years.

Breaking the Mould: Leaving the Nest: Her daring departure from "Charlie's Angels" demonstrated her desire for more creative freedom and a wider range of performing roles. The establishment of "Mother Productions" signalled a change in direction towards becoming a strong voice for female directors and producers.

Personal Struggles: Her balancing act became even more complex when she openedly addressed her addiction and mental health issues. She dispelled stigmas and encouraged others to accept vulnerability and ask for assistance by speaking up.

Diverse Achievements:

Activities: Kate's pursuits included producing and acting, but she also dabbled in directing, helming episodes of popular series like "Scarecrow and Mrs. King" and "Baby Boom," demonstrating her versatility.

Family and Philanthropy: She exhibited her ability to prioritise family and commit time to social impact by juggling her job with raising a family and actively supporting organisations such as St. Jude Children's Research Hospital and the Children's Miracle Network.

Subsequent Years: Environmental Advocacy: Her founding of the Environmental Media Association demonstrated her dedication to using her power for a more inclusive cause, striking a balance between her personal interests and the demands of society at large.

Sustained Advocacy: Kate continued to speak out about social concerns even after leaving the spotlight, displaying a lifetime commitment to changing the world via her words and deeds.

Lessons from Kate's Balance: Set your values first. Kate's story demonstrates how a more rewarding balance can result from coordinating your job with your passions and ideals.

Accept new challenges: In both your personal and professional life, don't be scared to venture outside of your comfort zone and try new things.

Kate Jackson

Speak up: Speak up for what you believe in, whether it be supporting societal causes that are important to you or yourself in your professional life.

Seek assistance: Creating a solid support system of friends, family, and mentors can be extremely beneficial in assisting you in overcoming life's unavoidable obstacles.

Embrace the path with joy: Remember that sustaining a lasting balance requires making time for the things that make you happy and improve your well-being.

Kate Jackson's life story provides an engaging viewpoint on maintaining balance in the face of a demanding work. We can all learn to master life's balancing act and build a fulfilling journey that aligns with our values and objectives by taking inspiration from her bravery, adaptability, and dedication to both personal and social issues.

Kate Jackson

5.1 Private Life

Like her business, Kate Jackson's personal life was complex, involving difficulties, grief, love, and ultimately, self-discovery.Here's an overview of the various currents she had to navigate:

Family and Romances:

Engagements and Marriages: Actor Andrew Stevens (with whom she adopted a son, Charles), businessman David Greenwald, and businessman Tom Hart were among the notable partnerships that Kate experienced during her life. She was also engaged to actor Edward Albert and producer Robert Evans. Despite the fact that some marriages ended in divorce, every chapter deepened her experience.

Motherhood and Adoption: After adopting Charles in 1995, Kate raised him as a single parent and experienced great joy and fulfilment in her life. Her activities and interviews demonstrate her unwavering commitment to being a mother.

Kate Jackson

Overcoming Obstacles:

Health Issues: Kate courageously battled breast cancer twice, receiving treatment and speaking out in favour of early identification and assistance for cancer sufferers. Many were encouraged by her candour on her challenges.

Financial Difficulties: Towards the end of her career, Kate experienced financial difficulties, proving that even celebrities can be vulnerable. She eventually overcame these obstacles by being resilient and independent.

Finding Balance and Self: Leaving the Spotlight: At the beginning of the new millennium, Kate made the decision to leave the spotlight, putting her personal life first and concentrating on her interests outside of Hollywood. This conscious decision to lead a peaceful life reveals a great deal about her view of her value as a person outside of the spotlight.

Personal Philanthropy: Kate demonstrated the true breadth of her compassion by helping at neighbourhood animal shelters and funding environmental projects while she was not in front of the cameras.

Teachings from Kate's Individual Experience:

Accept love and relationships: Although they don't always last, they can all improve our lives and provide important knowledge.

Put your family and loved ones first: Treasure the relationships you have with your loved ones because they act as a bulwark against life's storms.

Courageously confront obstacles: Life can be unpredictable, but by overcoming setbacks with fortitude and hope, one can utilise them as chances for personal development.

Never stop learning and developing: Life is alive and meaningful when one is always pursuing new passions and interests.

Find calm in the quiet: Taking a step back from the spotlight might help one become more self-aware and self-discovering.

Kate Jackson's private life wasn't always a glamorous, idealized story. It was a voyage full of highs and lows, successes and setbacks. But she made her own way through it all, putting her principles first, drawing strength from her vulnerabilities, and leaving a legacy of forbearance, self-acceptance, and perseverance.

Which particular facets of Kate's private life would you wish to learn more about? Maybe you're interested in learning about her adoption experiences, her approach to finding balance, or how she overcome obstacles. Depending on your particular interests, I'd be pleased to delve further into these topics and provide further insights.

5.3 Handling Hollywood Connections

Kate Jackson provided an intriguing look into the challenges of negotiating love and connection in the spotlight with her complex and nuanced romantic path through Hollywood. Here are some important themes to investigate:

Early Engagements and Romances:

Edward Albert: Her courtship with actor Edward Albert, which led to an engagement, attracted notice from the press and demonstrated her early yearning for a relationship.

Robert Evans: The decision to marry the influential producer signalled a change in focus towards achieving professional goals and negotiating the power structures in the business.

Andrew Stevens: The actor's marriage to her resulted in the adoption of their son, Charles, and the delight of motherhood. The value of family is illustrated in this chapter, even in the face of the pressures of a successful job.

Kate Jackson

Greenwald David and Hart Tom: The fact that Kate went on to marry businessman David Greenwald and then Tom Hart highlights her desire to find true love and companionship outside of the Hollywood bubble.

Obstacles and Fortitude:

Public Inquiry and Splits: Undoubtedly, the highly visible character of several of her relationships presented difficulties, since scrutiny and conjecture added a further level of complication to private affairs.

Sustaining Boundaries and Self-Worth: Resilience and the capacity to establish boundaries in order to safeguard one's emotional security and privacy were necessary for juggling a rigorous professional life with a personal life.

Relationship Lessons from Kate: Love and companionship can take many different shapes. Not every relationship has to have a set course or storyline. Each can offer growth, love, and priceless lessons.

Kate Jackson

Putting family and loved ones first: Regardless of the state of a relationship, having close relationships with family and friends provides support and stability.

Establishing limits and defending privacy: In the face of media attention, it's critical to learn how to handle criticism from the public and defend your personal space.

Discovering your value outside of relationships: Having a strong feeling of self-worth regardless of your romantic position requires you to acknowledge your strengths and value.

Gazing Past the Headlines:

Keep in mind that the most accurate perspectives on Kate's experiences come from her own words and deeds. Examining personal narratives, interviews, and her subsequent decisions to withdraw from public life can provide insight into her viewpoint on negotiating romantic relationships in Hollywood and placing mental health first.

Do you want to go more deeply into one particular area of Kate's relationships? Maybe you want to know how she handled the spotlight, how she balanced her personal and professional lives, or what she learned from her various relationships. I would be pleased to delve more into these topics and provide tailored analysis based on your own interests.

In the end, Kate's story serves as a helpful reminder that negotiating relationships in Hollywood—or any other industry—requires individuality and uniqueness. Every person has their own set of struggles and victories; the secret is to value oneself, accept vulnerability, and take lessons from both the good times and the bad along the road.

5.2 Individual Victories

Kate Jackson's life was a fabric of achievements that stretched much beyond the movie screen. Now let's examine a few of these outstanding accomplishments:

Kate Jackson

Breaking the Pattern: Introducing female producers: Resigning from "Charlie's Angels" and founding "Mother Productions" was a revolutionary decision that gave many actors the confidence and inspiration to take charge of their careers and reshape their roles in the business.

Empowered advocate: She smashed taboos, started crucial dialogues, and cleared the path for more acceptance and inclusion by using her position to support social justice causes including women's rights and LGBTQ+ equality.

Environmental activist: One of the most important things Hollywood did to encourage greener practices and increase public awareness of important environmental issues was to form the Environmental Media Association.

Outside the Spotlight: Overcoming Individual Challenges Kate broke stigmas and encouraged others to accept vulnerability and seek treatment by courageously and openly battling addiction and mental health issues.

Dedicated mother: She demonstrated her courage and commitment to family by lovingly and steadfastly adopting and rearing her son, Charles.

Unsung philanthropy: She showed a commitment to improving her neighbourhood even while it was hidden from the public by continuing to fund neighbourhood animal shelters, educational programmes, and environmental issues.

Beyond Notoriety: Inspiring a New Generation Artists, activists, and regular people are continually motivated to use their voices and take action for causes they believe in by Kate's unwavering commitment to social justice, environmental advocacy, and personal development.

Tangible legacies: She left behind organisations and policies that have a long-lasting influence on topics like cancer awareness, LGBTQ+ rights, and environmental sustainability.

Redefining success: Kate changed the definition of success via her experience. Her legacy serves as a reminder that genuine victories come from our positive effects on the world around us, not just from winning awards.

Examining Particular Victories:

Do you want to go into more detail on any particular aspect of Kate's victories? Maybe you're curious about the obstacles she had to overcome to break the mould in Hollywood, her effective advocacy tactics, or the endearing account of her devoted motherhood. Based on your particular interests, I'd be pleased to offer additional personalized insights.

5.3 The Point Where Fame and Intersection

The biography of Kate Jackson brilliantly illustrates the intriguing confluence of celebrity, advocacy, and personal development. Now let's unravel the strands of this complex tapestry:

Kate Jackson

Making the Most of Fame for Good:

Enhancing Underrepresented Voices: Kate championed
social justice causes like women's rights and LGBTQ+
equality by using her famous platform to raise awareness
and give voice to underrepresented groups.

Motivating others to become active in activism by
setting an example: Her personal support of
organisations like St. Jude Children's Research Hospital
and the Children's Miracle Network encouraged others to
do the same.

Bringing attention to environmental issues: Establishing
the Environmental Media Association demonstrated how
the power of celebrities to influence public opinion may
lead to important discussions and encourage the
entertainment sector to adopt sustainable practices.

Difficulties with Handling Public criticism: Juggling
Advocacy with Privacy: Kate had to manage public
criticism while promoting delicate concerns. It took
thoughtful deliberation and skillful communication to

strike the correct balance between one's personal life and public engagement.

Holding fast to her principles: Kate showed the significance of authenticity and integrity in the face of public pressure by holding fast to her ideals in the face of criticism and hostility.

Remaining focused on impact: Understanding that celebrity can have both positive and negative effects, Kate made sure to concentrate on the real change she wanted to see via her advocacy rather than just the attention it received.

Personal Development Outside the Lens:

Discovering fulfilment and self-expression: Kate's decision to leave Hollywood behind and pursue her passions outside of the spotlight showed that true fulfilment can come from pursuing interests and artistic endeavours outside of the entertainment industry.

Kate Jackson

Putting inner serenity and well-being first: Overcoming personal challenges like addiction and accepting vulnerability shown that, despite one's public image, personal development and recovery are essential for long-lasting happiness.

Making an impact in her community: Kate demonstrated the value of persistent dedication to causes one cares about by being involved in neighbourhood philanthropy and environmental projects even after stepping back from the spotlight.

Takeaways from the Crossroads:

Celebrity may be a potent force for good in society: Celebrity influence may elevate important perspectives and have a beneficial impact when used sensibly and sincerely.

Activism demands bravery and tenacity: It can be difficult to stand up for what you believe in, but Kate's story highlights the benefits of tenacity and moral integrity.

Kate Jackson

The secret to long-lasting fulfilment is personal growth: A meaningful life requires putting your health first and pursuing your passions, whether or not you are in the spotlight.

Examining Particular Crossroads:

Which particular facets of Kate's life at the crossroads of action and celebrity particularly interest you? Maybe you want to know how she handled backlash for her activism, how she made the most of her famous power, or how she found fulfilment in life outside of the spotlight. Based on your particular interests, I'd be pleased to offer additional in-depth information.

Kate's narrative demonstrates that celebrity does not define an individual or the impact they can make. It is a tool that can be used to draw attention to crucial problems, give voices to those who cannot be heard, and spur action.

CHAPTER 6: FROM SCREEN TO ACTIVISM

The path of Kate Jackson goes beyond the realm of Hollywood glitz. It's a compelling tale of an angelic transformation that takes off not only on screen but also on the wings of activism.

The initial spark of advocacy:

Though Kate was a "Charlie's Angels" fan, her social conscience was always there. Her outspoken criticism of sexism and support of gender equality laid the groundwork for her future action.

Her early determination to use her position for constructive change was demonstrated by her work with organisations such as the Feminist Majority Foundation, which further established her dedication to social justice.

Beyond Pleasure: Accepting Activism:

Kate Jackson

After escaping Hollywood, Kate founded "Mother Productions," which served as both a launchpad for her artistic and activism goals and a production company.

A significant change was the founding of the Environmental Media Association. It brought the entertainment sector together with environmental causes, raising awareness and promoting environmentally friendly behaviours.

Promoting a Range of Causes:

Kate did not advocate for just one cause. She gave voice to a wide range of causes, including LGBTQ+ rights, fighting prejudice and promoting acceptance, as well as children's welfare through institutions like the Children's Miracle Network and St. Jude Children's Research Hospital.

Her candour about her struggles with addiction and mental health problems turned into a potent weapon for shattering stigmas and inspiring others to get treatment.

Kate Jackson

Moving Past Visibility and Towards Action: Kate wasn't satisfied with awareness alone. She made sure her advocacy resulted in real action and constructive change by planning, coordinating, and actively participating in events like rallies and campaigns.

Her passion to making a difference outside of the big stages was demonstrated by her efforts to support smaller communities through animal welfare and educational programmes.

The Legacy of Transformation: A generation of people are motivated by Kate's story to view themselves as change agents as well as entertainment consumers.

Her efforts with the EMA continue to impact Hollywood's environmental impact, and her support of social justice opens doors for increased acceptance and inclusivity.

Most significantly, she serves as a reminder that anyone can effect change without the help of a celebrity platform. Every word spoken and every action taken has the capacity to have a good knock-on effect.

6.1 Kate's Influence

Kate Jackson has had a profound influence on social justice, sustainability, and self-awareness that goes well beyond the flash and glamour of Hollywood. Here's a closer look at her diverse influence:

Promoting Social Justice:

Women's Rights: Kate's outspoken support of gender equality dispelled myths and opened doors for more women to be represented and given opportunities in both society and Hollywood.

LGBTQ+ Parity: Her steadfast advocacy for LGBTQ+ rights during a period of intense discrimination paved the way for future advancements by fostering a deeper sense of acceptance and understanding.

Kate Jackson

Children's Welfare: A commitment to working with organisations such as St. Jude Children's Research Hospital and the Children's Miracle Network resulted in real benefits for a great number of ill and damaged kids.

Environmental Hero: Establishing the Environmental Media Association: This historic move sparked real action in the entertainment sector by promoting sustainable practices and influencing production techniques, in addition to increasing public awareness of environmental issues.

Inspiring Change: Kate's stardom spurred the green movement by inspiring millions of followers and Hollywood peers to talk and take action.

Leaving a Legacy: As evidence of Kate's enduring influence, the EMA is still thriving and has a significant impact on environmental awareness and practices in the entertainment sector.

Personal Development and Vulnerability: Honestly Facing Addiction and Mental Health: Kate's bravery in facing her personal issues broke down barriers and encouraged others to get treatment, starting crucial discussions about mental health assistance and awareness.

Motivating Self-Acceptance: She inspired others to embrace their vulnerabilities and place a higher priority on personal growth than outside pressures by sharing her journey of self-discovery and well-being.

Redefining Success: Kate valued impact, honesty, and personal fulfilment in addition to celebrity and honours. Her concept of success speaks to those who are looking for meaning and purpose in their life.

Impact of Inspiration Ripples:

Empowering Individuals: Kate's story inspires people to speak up for issues they support, find their own voices, and make a difference—no matter how tiny.

Inspiring Conversations: Her activism sparked important discussions about social justice, the environment, and individual wellbeing. As a result, it had a lasting impact on public opinion and helped to shape attitudes.

Leaving a Legacy of Action: By encouraging future generations to be change agents and contribute to a more equitable and sustainable world, Kate's life acts as a call to action.

Kate's influence is a living legacy that uplifts and empowers people today, not just a historical anecdote.

6.2 Breaking New Ground in the Entertainment Sector

Kate Jackson is a trailblazer in the entertainment industry who has left a lasting impact on the industry as a whole as well as the art form.

Smashing the Mould: From Angel to Executive: She broke free from the constraints imposed on actresses at the time by forming "Mother Productions" and stepping away from the "Charlie's Angels" spotlight.

Kate Jackson

Supporting Female Creatives: In a field dominated by men, Kate cleared the path for other women to take charge of their stories and assert their creative authority.

Challenging Stereotypes: She pushed for more realistic and nuanced depictions of women in Hollywood by challenging the stereotypes surrounding them through her advocacy and varied roles.

Using her Platform to Make an Impact: Kate wasn't afraid to utilise her notoriety to promote social and environmental problems, encouraging others to speak up and call for change.

Establishing the Environmental Media Association: This ground-breaking project brought the environmental movement and Hollywood together, promoting sustainable practices and increasing public awareness of important concerns.

Fighting for Equality: She broke down barriers and cleared the way for more diversity in the industry by vocally supporting topics like women's rights and LGBTQ+ equality.

Setting a Good Example:

Embracing Vulnerability: By being honest about her own battles with addiction and mental illness, Kate questioned the Hollywood ideal of perfection and inspired people to accept who they are flaws and all.

Putting Health First: Retaining the spotlight while concentrating on personal development showed how important self-care and mental wellness are in a tough field.

Leaving a Legacy of Inspiration: In spite of industry pressures, Kate's story continues to encourage ambitious actors, producers, and activists to pursue their dreams, stand up for what they believe in, and put their health first.

Kate Jackson

6.3 Aims for Women's Empowerment

Kate Jackson's influence on female empowerment extended beyond her well-known cinematic appearances. Taking a closer look at the ways she promoted the cause is as follows:

Smashing Preconceptions:

Past the Angel: Actresses' constraints were broken as they stepped away from "Charlie's Angels" to explore varied parts, opening the door for more complex and realistic representations of women.

Mother Productions: By starting her own production business, she gave creative authority to other female creatives and challenged the male-dominated industry.

Speaking Up: Kate furthered the challenge to industry conventions and created significant conversations with her outspoken support for gender equality in interviews and public forums.

Kate Jackson

Shattering Barriers: Importance of Representation A generation was motivated to see greater possibilities for themselves by strong, independent women who played a variety of roles, from formidable lawyers to sci-fi heroes.

Championing Female Creatives: Kate broke down barriers and pushed for diversity in the business by actively working with and supporting female directors, writers, and producers.

Role Model and Mentor: She encouraged a mentorship and support culture in the community by candidly sharing her experiences and offering advice to young actors.

Motivating Action: Using her Platform: Kate made use of her notoriety to support feminist groups like the Feminist Majority Foundation, giving their voices more weight and expanding their audience.

The Power of Collective Action: Participating in campaigns, rallies, and fundraising events with other women demonstrated the significance of unity and group action in bringing about change.

Personal Development and Vulnerability: By accepting and candidly discussing her personal challenges, she fought against the ideal of perfection and inspired other women to put their health first and accept who they really are.

Legacy of Empowerment: Kate's story continues to motivate females to fight for equal rights in all areas of life, follow their passions, and confront stereotypes.

Her commitment to mentoring and diversity created a welcoming environment in the entertainment industry and opened the door for more women to work together and be represented.

Above all, she showed that empowerment doesn't need a spotlight. Every voice, every action, and every decision to be authentically oneself adds up to a force for good in society.

Kate's narrative serves as a call to action for all women, not just those working in the entertainment sector. Her bravery, dedication, and unflinching faith in the ability of women to build a more just and empowering future serve as examples for all of us.

Let's keep pushing for the things she believed in, dismantling obstacles in our way, and standing by one another as we strive for equality and opportunity. By working together, we can continue Kate's legacy and create a global empowerment fabric that helps women everywhere.

6.4 Motivating the Next Generation

A tribute to the continuing power of passion, fortitude, and the desire to make a difference, Kate Jackson's journey serves as a beacon of inspiration for a new generation. Let's examine the ways in which her legacy continues to stoke young people's dreams and imaginations:

Kate Jackson

Shaking Up the Game and Exceeding Predictions: From Guardian to Supporter Kate's journey from Hollywood actress to committed activist serves as a reminder of the value of defying convention and pursuing interests outside of the box. A generation that wants to define success according to their own standards can relate to this.

Accepting Vulnerability and Imperfection: Her candour on her own battles with addiction and mental illness normalises human frailty and inspires youth to put their health first and seek help without feeling guilty.

Paving the Way for Diverse perspectives: Kate championed marginalised perspectives and encourages a new generation to fight for social justice and inclusivity. She is an advocate for women's rights, LGBTQ+ equality, and sustainability.

Developing the Future Generation:

Championing Female Creatives: Kate exemplifies the value of mentorship and providing a platform for marginalised voices by founding "Mother Productions" and helping other women in the business. Young women are encouraged to follow their aspirations of being leaders and creatives by this.

Activism Beyond the Spotlight: Putting less emphasis on Hollywood and more on neighbourhood charity and community involvement serves to bolster the idea that significant change can occur anywhere, not only on large stages. This gives youth the ability to change their local communities.

Leaving a Legacy of Action: Kate co-founded the Environmental Media Association, an organisation that is still strong today, providing observable evidence of the long-term benefits of activism and encouraging future generations of activists.

Finding Inspiration in Kate's Journey: Kate's bravery in defying social standards and pursuing her passions might serve as an example for young people aspiring to forge their own pathways.

Kate Jackson

Her honesty and fortitude will be a source of strength for anyone facing personal struggles, and her tale of triumphing over hardship will inspire hope.

Aspiring activists can get insight into the power of collective action and amplify marginalised voices by studying her strategic approach to lobbying.

Taking the Torch: Kate Leaves a Vibrant Call to Action, Not a Museum Exhibit. Her life serves as an example for all of us to follow in order to embrace our unique passions and make the world more equitable and sustainable.

Dispel myths and stand up for people whose voices deserve to be heard.Encourage and empower one another to build a network of empathy and group effort.

Kate's tale serves as a reminder that everyone has the ability to make their own impact on the world, not simply one woman's accomplishments. We can all help create a better future for ourselves and future generations by continuing her advocacy, empathy, and self-discovery.

Kate Jackson

CHAPTER 7: LIFE LESSONS

1. Resilience in the Face of Challenges: Kate exemplifies resilience by being candid about her struggle with breast cancer. She overcame personal hardship and used her story to encourage and uplift others.

2. Adaptability and Versatility: Kate demonstrated her flexibility in roles such as "Scarecrow and Mrs. King" and "Charlie's Angels." Her openness to taking on a variety of responsibilities illustrates how crucial flexibility is for managing a fast-paced professional environment.

3. Female Empowerment in Representation: Kate's roles dispelled preconceptions by showcasing women as capable, self-reliant, and clever. The ability to question conventions and support good representation is the lesson to be learned from this.

4. Dedication to Personal Development: Kate's path into producing and directing represents a dedication to

ongoing personal and professional development. It highlights how crucial it is to develop and broaden one's skill set.

5. Inspiration to Tell Personal Tales: Kate showed how vulnerability can be a source of strength by discussing her health struggle. The lesson lies in the value of genuineness and the way that people can be moved and motivated by one another's experiences.

6. Active Involvement in Advocacy: Kate's efforts to raise awareness of breast cancer demonstrate the value of utilizing one's position to further a cause. Leveraging influence to constructively impact societal challenges is the lesson to be learned.

7. Halving Glamour with Substance: Kate's professional background demonstrates that achievement may transcend outward glamour.Deepness, substance, and a dedication to purposeful narrative all go into creating a legacy that is unforgettable.

To put it briefly, Kate Jackson's life lessons are applicable not only to the entertainment industry but also provide insightful guidance for anyone facing the challenges of both personal and professional development.

7.1 Examining Kate Jackson's career

Kate Jackson's career highlights a complex path characterized by adaptability, cultural influence, and inner fortitude. Kate's versatility in portraying a range of characters demonstrated her depth as an actress, from her classic performance as Sabrina Duncan in "Charlie's Angels" to her subsequent contributions in "Scarecrow and Mrs. King" and beyond.

Her impact is felt off screen as well, especially given how candid she is about overcoming personal obstacles like breast cancer. This openness showed a willingness to be vulnerable as well as a dedication to bringing attention to and helping those who are struggling with their health.

Kate Jackson

When one considers Kate Jackson's career, one must acknowledge her pioneering role in changing the way women are portrayed on television. Her characters contributed to a more progressive narrative in the entertainment industry by being smart, strong, and gorgeous women.

Her path into producing and directing also demonstrated a strong willingness to actively participate in the storytelling process and a dynamic engagement with the dynamically changing entertainment industry.

Kate Jackson's observations essentially tell the story of her personal and professional development, resiliency, and dedication to honesty. Her advocacy work and the path she paved for upcoming generations in the entertainment industry are just as significant as the characters she brought to life.

7.2 Knowledge Acquired by Experience

Experienced wisdom frequently entails taking lessons from both setbacks and victories. In Kate Jackson's case,

Kate Jackson

her experience in the entertainment business probably gave her valuable lessons about tenacity, dealing with uncertainty, and the value of ongoing personal development.

Kate Jackson's autobiographical journey is replete with lessons about growth, resiliency, and the pursuit of authenticity. Kate managed the difficulties of celebrity and personal development throughout her career, from her early days in the entertainment business to her latter pursuits.

Kate faced the highs and lows of popularity while playing Sabrina Duncan in "Charlie's Angels," her breakthrough role. This was the start of her self-discovery adventure, during which she built her public persona while delving into the vibrant world of Hollywood.

Kate's career took a turn in the 1980s when she starred in "Scarecrow and Mrs. King," which revealed a new side to her acting abilities.This stage not only showed off her variety but also suggested that she would be delving further into her profession and committing to roles that truly spoke to her.

Over the years, Kate's career branched out into directing and producing in addition to performing. This broadening of her artistic boundaries revealed a lady who was eager to learn more about the field and about herself. It was a voyage that revealed a dedication to artistic discovery and a resolve to add to storytelling from a variety of perspectives, behind the surface glamour.

In addition to her career triumphs, Kate Jackson's personal struggles with health gave depth to her story of self-discovery. Her candour regarding difficulties served as both a sign of her sincerity and an inspiration to others going through comparable difficulties.

Looking back, Kate Jackson's self-discovery journey is not limited to a particular time period or character; rather, it is a continuous story. It's a tale of resiliency, reinvention, and the never-ending search for genuineness in a society that frequently rewards conformity.

Kate serves as a constant reminder that the process of self-discovery is dynamic and transformative, mirroring the depth and nuance of the characters she so skillfully brought to life on film.

7.3 The Legacy Continue

In the future, Kate Jackson's legacy is expected to continue serving as a source of motivation and impact. The lessons she learned about resilience, adaptability, and a dedication to authenticity will be valuable to budding performers and others going through difficult times in their lives.

Future generations of storytellers will probably be inspired by Kate's trailblazing attitude and influence on female representation in the entertainment business as it develops. The continued movement in favor of varied stories and the understanding of the value of genuineness are consistent with the values she upheld throughout her professional life.

Furthermore, Kate's contributions to health awareness and societal challenges are likely to continue to have a positive impact if she stays active in advocacy and philanthropy. The stories she told and the work she did will always have an impact and leave a legacy that will last beyond time.

Looking ahead, people negotiating the challenges of life and work can find inspiration from Kate Jackson's journey. Her legacy exemplifies the notion that one's own development, resiliency, and dedication to changing the world have an enduring and significant impression.

CHAPTER 8: SILVER SCREEN SUCCESS

A pivotal moment in Kate Jackson's illustrious career was her foray onto the silver screen. Despite the fact that television was her primary source of recognition, her film debut showcased her adaptability to several storytelling forms.

Kate Jackson's acting career extended beyond television with roles in films like "Thunder and Lightning" (1977) and "Making Love" (1982). These parts gave her the chance to experiment with a variety of genres, from drama to action comedy, demonstrating her ability to flourish in a range of cinematic settings.

Her accomplishments on the silver screen enhanced her professional portfolio and offered context to the story of her influence on the entertainment industry as a whole.

Kate's versatility as an actor was demonstrated by her ability to switch between television and films, which further cemented her place as a significant player in the Hollywood industry.

In retrospect, Kate Jackson's triumph on the silver screen is evidence of her lasting charm and creative versatility, demonstrating her capacity to enthrall viewers on TV and in films.

8.1 The Development of Kate's Trade

Over her career, Kate Jackson's craft underwent substantial evolution. She displayed a blend of intelligence and charisma starting in the 1970s with her breakthrough performance as Sabrina Duncan in "Charlie's Angels." Her ability to capture a variety of emotions, from action sequences to more subtle character changes, improved as the series went on.

Throughout the 1980s, Kate continued to widen her horizons by accepting challenging roles in films and television series. The way she merged dramatic and romantic elements in "Scarecrow and Mrs. King" as Amanda King showed off her flexibility.

Kate's skill set was further developed later in her career when she tried her hand at producing and directing. This change demonstrates her acting talent as well as her thorough knowledge of the business.It indicates a yearning for artistic freedom and a readiness to do more than just act in a story.

All things considered, Kate Jackson's career has developed through her unwavering pursuit of personal development, acceptance of a variety of roles, and extension of her impact in the entertainment industry.

8.2 Identifying

Beyond her nominations for Emmy Awards and Golden Globes, Kate Jackson's impact went beyond accolades. She became well-known during the "Charlie's Angels" era due to her enormous cultural influence.

Her portrayal of Sabrina Duncan left an enduring effect on television history, and the show's popularity was greatly aided by the connection she had with her co-stars.

Kate's recognition was further enhanced by her advocacy work, particularly her efforts to raise awareness about breast cancer. Her own experience with the illness and her subsequent devotion to activism shown her fortitude and resolve to have a good influence outside of the entertainment industry.

Even if accolades are a material kind of acknowledgment, Kate Jackson's ongoing appeal, cultural impact, and charity donations all serve to reinforce her standing as a reputable member of the entertainment world.

8.3 Honors

Kate Jackson was praised by critics and nominated for awards for her exceptional performance in television, especially on "Charlie's Angels" and "Scarecrow and Mrs. King.

1. Emmy Awards: For her performance as Sabrina Duncan in "Charlie's Angels" in the late 1970s, Kate Jackson was nominated for four Primetime Emmy

Kate Jackson

Awards, including Outstanding Lead Actress in a Drama
Series.

2. Golden Globe Awards: Her portrayal of Amanda King
in "Scarecrow and Mrs. King" garnered her a nomination
for Best Actress in a Television Series, Drama at the
Golden Globes.

3. Other Recognitions: Although she was not the winner
of these honors, the nominations show that the television
industry recognized her talent and contribution.

Beyond accolades, Kate Jackson's influence may be seen
in popular culture as one of the famous television faces
of the 1970s and 1980s. Her enduring presence in the
entertainment business can be attributed to her impact on
the detective genre and her talent for giving her
characters nuance.

8.4 Contributions to the Motion Picture

Even though Kate Jackson's career on television is more
well-known, her work in films demonstrates her

adaptability and desire to take on different roles. Further information about her contributions on the silver screen is as follows:

1. "Making Love" (1982): Kate portrayed Claire in this ground-breaking movie, a woman negotiating the difficulties of a changing marriage.She was able to take on increasingly complex and emotionally sophisticated parts as the movie tackled themes of relationships and sexuality.

2. "Thunder and Lightning" (1977): Kate Jackson was able to venture into a new genre with this action-comedy movie. Alongside David Carradine, her portrayal as Nancy Sue Hunnicutt showcased her adaptability and readiness to take on parts that were fun and adventurous.

3. Exploration of Genres: Kate's cinematic endeavors showcased her aim to broaden her range of work. Her choice of roles demonstrated her versatility, as she was able to transition between comedic and dramatic roles,

even though her cinema career may not have been as long as her television one.

4. Creative Involvement: Kate Jackson's contribution to the movie went beyond her performance as an actor. Her curiosity about the creative process inspired her to investigate producing and directing, which helped to shape the entertainment industry's overall structure.

Even though Kate Jackson's success in film may not have been as great as it was on television, her contributions to the medium have enhanced her artistic legacy. Her openness to embracing various genres is a testament to her dedication to development and creative inquiry.

8.5 TV

Even if Kate Jackson's success on television may have been greater than her film career, her noteworthy contributions to the film industry gave her artistic repertory more depth:

Kate Jackson

1. "Loverboy" (1989): Kate Jackson portrayed Diane Bodek in this romantic comedy picture. The movie looks at romance and relationships, and it shows off how charming and warm she is on the big screen.

2. "Clean and Narrow" (1999): Jackson played the part of Carol in this criminal drama film. She gets the chance to play a character with nuance as the film explores the nuances of family connections in the setting of crime and justice.

3. Diversity in Roles: Kate Jackson's dedication to diversity was evident in her cinematic roles. She experimented with several genres, showcasing her flexibility as an actress, ranging from criminal dramas to romantic comedies.

4. Behind the Scenes: Kate Jackson's passion for filmmaking prompted her to consider positions behind the camera in addition to performing. Her involvement in directing and producing films demonstrates a diverse approach to the business.

Kate Jackson

Although Kate Jackson's filmography may not be as substantial as her television work, her contributions to the medium show her versatility and ongoing study of many storytelling formats. Her on-screen persona contributed significant depth to her long-lasting reputation in the entertainment industry.

CHAPTER 9: HOLLYWOOD'S CHANGING LANDSCAPE

Recent years have seen substantial changes to Hollywood's landscape, with a number of noteworthy movements influencing the sector:

1. Diversity and Inclusion: Diversity and inclusion, both in front of and behind the camera, are becoming increasingly important in Hollywood. Storytelling that is more inclusive is a result of a greater understanding of the need for greater representation of race, gender, and other identities.

2. Dominance of Streaming Services: The emergence of streaming services has changed how people watch media. Streaming services like Netflix, Hulu, and Disney+ have grown to be significant participants in the film industry, upending established studio structures and changing the creation, release, and consumption of films and television shows.

Kate Jackson

3. Digital Effects and Technology: The film industry has undergone a revolution thanks to technological breakthroughs, especially in the areas of digital effects and virtual production. This has altered the way filmmakers approach storytelling and visual effects and opened them new creative avenues.

4. Modifying Distribution Frameworks: There have been difficulties with the conventional theatrical release paradigm, particularly in light of the COVID-19 epidemic. In order to have greater flexibility in reaching audiences, studios are investigating hybrid release tactics that combine digital distribution with theatrical releases.

5. Impact of Social Media: Social media is now a potent instrument for audience engagement and marketing. A movie's reception is largely influenced by social media buzz, fan interaction, and online reviews in addition to box office receipts.

6. Changes in Preferences for Genres: Popular films have changed due to shifting audience preferences.

Diverse genres, such as indie films, documentaries, and foreign films, are becoming more and more popular, which reflects a wider diversity of tastes in narrative.

7. Focus on Original Content: The creation of original content in Hollywood has increased dramatically, with an emphasis on original and creative storytelling. To draw users, streaming services, in particular, spend a lot of money producing unique, exclusive content.

These developments add to a dynamic and always-shifting Hollywood scene, influencing the direction of the entertainment sector going forward.

9.1 Notes on Changes in the Industry

Several significant developments that have recently changed the entertainment scene can be seen by observing the changes in the sector:

1. New Creative Platforms Emerging: Platforms like YouTube, TikTok, and other social media have grown to be effective avenues for creative expression in addition

to conventional film and television. Gatekeepers from the old industry are no longer necessary for independent creators to reach consumers around the world.

2. Impact of Globalization: With filmmakers and content creators from many nations obtaining prominence, the business has grown more international. An increasingly integrated global entertainment environment has been made possible by international collaborations, diversified storytelling, and the accessibility of content across national boundaries.

3. Fan Engagement's Influence: TV series and films are greatly influenced by social media and online fan communities. Fan-driven campaigns can impact decisions, such as bringing back canceled shows or altering creative paths in response to audience preferences. Studios are increasingly taking into account comments from fans.

4. The Ascent of Franchise Cinemas:

Franchise-driven narrative, frequently observed in fantasy and superhero categories, has emerged as a powerful influence. To maintain audience engagement over time and foster brand loyalty, studios make investments in developing interconnected universes.

5. Tech-Driven Innovations: The audience experience is being improved and narrative methods are being influenced by technological breakthroughs such as augmented reality (AR), virtual reality (VR), and artificial intelligence (AI). These developments create new avenues for interactive and immersive storytelling.

6. Difficulties with Conventional Distribution Strategies: Streaming platforms are posing a threat to theatrical releases, which is having an effect on conventional distribution strategies. Some films are choosing to have simultaneous or exclusive digital releases as a result of studios reevaluating their release methods.

7. Business Reaction to Social Concerns: With a rising emphasis on diversity, representation, and tackling social

themes in storytelling, the industry is becoming more sensitive to societal issues. This is indicative of a larger trend in society that demands content that is more socially conscious and responsible.

8. Traversing the Pandemic's Effects: The industry has seen rapid changes as a result of the COVID-19 epidemic, including a greater emphasis on digital platforms, remote productions, and hybrid distribution formats. The way content is produced, shared, and consumed has changed as a result of these modifications.

These insights demonstrate how quickly the entertainment sector is changing as a result of global, cultural, and technical changes that are redefining how people tell and enjoy tales.

9.2 Originality

The inventiveness of Kate Jackson can be found in the way she pioneered female roles in television during a period of radical change. As one of the first "Charlie's

Kate Jackson

Angels," she helped dispel preconceived notions about gender.

The show, which changed the way women were portrayed on television, was well-known for its uplifting depictions of women in roles of crime-solving.

Sabrina Duncan, played by Jackson, was more than simply a glamorous sidekick; she was a perceptive, competent, and self-sufficient investigator.

This innovation provided a more progressive and powerful story, challenging the traditional norms of women's roles in the media.

 The popularity of "Charlie's Angels" helped to change how the industry saw women on television in general and paved the way for other female-led action shows in the future.

Kate Jackson's influence on television signified a cultural and narrative innovation that opened the door for more varied and powerful female characters in the entertainment business, even though it was not directly related to technology advancement. Her input is in line with a larger narrative shift in how women are portrayed on television.

9.3 Guiding the Upcoming Generation

In each sector, including entertainment, nurturing development and continuity requires mentoring the next generation. I'm not aware of any specifics of Kate Jackson's mentoring activities, but in the entertainment industry, mentoring is crucial. It entails seasoned professionals imparting expertise, advice, and insights to up-and-coming talent.

If Kate Jackson has mentored others, it probably entails sharing knowledge acquired from her own experience, giving guidance on negotiating the difficulties of the field, and offering encouragement to those who aspire to be like her.

The process of mentoring is an effective way to impart both hard talents and soft skills that lead to success, such

Kate Jackson

as perseverance, adaptability, and a dedication to lifelong learning.

CHAPTER 10: KATE'S CHARITABLE ENDEAVOR

Through her unwavering humanitarian endeavors, Kate Jackson, the legendary actress best remembered for her appearances in Scarecrow and Mrs. King and Charlie's Angels, has not only left her stamp on television history but also on the world.

Her work has involved supporting a wide range of issues using her voice and resources, changing the lives of innumerable people.

Promoting Awareness of Breast Cancer:

Kate became passionate about promoting for early detection and research after going through a personal struggle with breast cancer in the early 1990s. She rose to prominence as a spokesperson for a number of organisations, including Susan G. Komen and the American Cancer Society, encouraging people to battle cancer by increasing awareness of the illness.

Kate Jackson

Battling for Animal Welfare: Kate has always had a strong passion for animals, which is demonstrated by her involvement with groups like PETA and the American Humane Association. She vigorously backs initiatives to stop animal abuse, encourages responsible pet ownership, and supports environmental preservation.

Investing in Youth Development and Education: Kate is a supporter of Save the Children and UNICEF because she understands the power of education to shape the future. She makes contributions to initiatives that give disadvantaged kids throughout the globe access to education, inspiring hope and enabling them to realise their full potential.

Environmental Champion: Kate is a strong supporter of environmental conservation because she recognises the vital role that safeguarding the environment plays. Her support for groups that promote sustainable practices and increase public awareness of environmental issues includes the Nature Conservancy and Greenpeace.

Kate Jackson

Beyond Organisations: In addition to her work with well-known organisations, Kate uses her position and connections to advocate for causes and nonprofits that are dear to her. She contributes her voice to campaigns, takes part in fundraising events, and uses social media to inform and motivate people to become engaged.

Kate's Charitable Legacy:

Kate Jackson is a philanthropist who does much more than just provide money. She gives each cause she supports her wholehearted devotion, time, and enthusiasm, genuinely improving the lives of those in need. Others in the entertainment business and beyond are inspired by her unwavering passion and are encouraged to use their power for good.

Continuing the Journey: Kate Jackson is still actively involved in a number of humanitarian endeavors at the age of 74.

Her narrative is a potent reminder that contributing to society can take a lifetime, with the potential to leave a lasting legacy that extends well beyond the stage or screen.

We can inspire people to follow their own charitable pathways and act as change agents in their communities by sharing her inspirational achievements.

Recall that this is only the beginning! Please feel free to delve deeper into any of the causes Kate has backed, offer firsthand accounts of her involvement, or even highlight any planned activities in which she may be involved. Together, we can continue to draw attention to her kind giving and encourage others to do the same.

10.1 Laying the Groundwork

Once associated with legendary television parts, Kate Jackson is now a supporter of causes outside of the entertainment industry. Her relentless commitment to give back and changing the world in a meaningful way is what motivates her to build enduring change foundations.

Kate Jackson

A Foundation of Oneself: Overcoming Adversity Kate's personal experience with breast cancer in the early 1990s served as inspiration for her fervent support of healthcare reform. Her advocacy for early detection and research activities through organizations like the American Cancer Society and Susan G. Komen was sparked by this personal experience.

Creating Change-Building Structures: Supporting Causes Near and Dear to Her Heart: Kate's generosity goes much beyond medical aid. She created or actively advocates for a number of foundations that provide devoted assistance to a broad range of causes:

Animal Welfare: Kate's dedication to combating animal abuse and encouraging ethical pet ownership is evident in her involvement with groups like PETA and the American Humane Association.

Education and Youth Development: Kate invests in organisations like Save the Children and UNICEF, giving impoverished children worldwide opportunity, since she recognises the transforming potential of education.

Environmental Conservation: Kate actively supports organisations like the Nature Conservancy and Greenpeace, pushing for sustainable practices and increasing awareness about environmental challenges, because she recognises the need of saving our planet.

Beyond Physical Stores: Using Perception to Make an Impact Kate is devoted in ways that go beyond material support. She uses her voice and platform to support important causes, encourage action, and increase awareness. Her social media presence turns into an instrument for involvement and education, inspiring people to support the causes she is deeply committed to.

As the Legacy Develops: A Pioneer in Philanthropic ActionKate Jackson's path is a compelling illustration of how perseverance and unshakable commitment may lead to long-lasting change. She establishes the groundwork for a future in which her influence will last for generations by laying a variety of foundations, including personal, organisational, and community-based ones.

What Comes Next:

Going Further: There is more to learn about each of Kate's selected causes: go into greater detail about particular projects she backs, present moving accounts of lives she has impacted, or highlight forthcoming events in which she will participate.

Examine how Kate's efforts encourage others to become engaged by conducting interviews with volunteers, highlighting the experiences of neighbourhood heroes who are improving their neighbourhoods, or showcasing projects that are motivated by her commitment.

Beyond the Spotlight: Talk about the value of taking individual action, the significance of community involvement, and the opportunities and problems encountered in diverse philanthropic sectors. Go beyond celebrity philanthropy and relate Kate's efforts to more significant social issues.

Kate Jackson

Kate Jackson's legacy extends beyond a CV of humanitarian endeavours. It is evidence of the strength of self-improvement, committed effort, and persistent devotion. via an examination of the foundations she has built, both internally and via her unwavering work, we may honor her influence and encourage others to forge their own charitable legacies.

10.2 Working Together with Nonprofits

Kate Jackson's genuine genius is evident in her unwavering commitment to social change, which shows through even in the bright lights and legendary parts. She advocates causes important to her heart through a tapestry of partnerships with various NGOs, making a lasting impact on the lives of innumerable people as well as the world itself.

Getting Over Personal Challenges to Effective Advocacy: Overcoming Adversity Kate was driven by her own experience with breast cancer in the early 1990s. As a result of her partnerships with groups like

Kate Jackson

Susan G. Komen and the American Cancer Society, she developed into a tenacious supporter of early detection and research, her voice blazing the way to a better future for individuals facing the illness.

Fostering Animal Welfare and Safeguarding Our Furry Friends: Kate has an unwavering passion for animals. Together with the American Humane Association and PETA, she combats animal abuse, encourages responsible pet ownership, and cultivates compassion for all living things, no matter how big or small. Her steadfast compassion opens the door to a more compassionate world for our animal friends.

Developing Future Builders: Taking Care of Young Minds Understanding the transformational potential of education, Kate works with UNICEF and Save the Children, among other organisations. Through her work, impoverished children all throughout the world can receive high-quality education, giving them the skills they need to create better futures for themselves and their communities.

Kate Jackson

Preserving Our Precious Planet: Ecological Management
Kate works tirelessly to promote environmental
conservation through partnerships with Greenpeace and
the Nature Conservancy. Her voice reflects the urgency
of preserving the environment, promoting sustainable
lifestyles, and bringing important environmental issues
to public attention.

Beyond Monetary Assistance: Strengthening Voices:
Kate's influence goes well beyond her material efforts.
She uses her position and power to encourage action,
spread awareness, and give voice to the concerns of
those who are frequently ignored. She encourages others
to support the causes she supports by lighting a flame of
change through her public appearances and social media
presence.

Working Together: A Spark for Change:

Synergy for Good: Every charity partnership produces a
special synergy that amplifies the effect of each person's
work.Kate is aware of this influence and uses it to her

advantage when forming alliances that bring together a range of skills and resources to address difficult problems and produce ground-breaking outcomes.

A Beacon of Hope: Motivating a Generation: Kate's story acts as a motivator for a new generation to embrace charity and support topics they are passionate about. Her unceasing efforts show that one individual may have a profound impact via committed teamwork.

The Tapestry Opens Up:

Go Further: Examine particular projects that Kate backs via her partnerships, provide personal tales of people who have benefited from her efforts, or highlight forthcoming events in which she will be present.

Past the Glare: Talk about the opportunities and difficulties encountered in nonprofit collaborations, and how overcoming these barriers results in a bigger effect.

Join the Dots: Describe how Kate's partnerships help society achieve more general objectives, like the

Sustainable Development Goals or the advancement of social justice movements.

The story of Kate Jackson is about more than just celebrity philanthropy; it's about the strength of teamwork, commitment, and steadfast faith in a brighter future. By learning more about the rich tapestry of her charitable partnerships, we may honor her accomplishments, rekindle our own passions for social change, and create a more promising future for future generations.

10.3 The Effects of Volunteering

Though the name Kate Jackson may evoke visions of Scarecrow and Mrs. King or Charlie's Angels, behind the scenes is a woman whose influence reaches well beyond the big screen. Kate's legacy is shaped by her unwavering commitment to giving back and changing the world, not just by her acting prowess.

From Internal Conflicts to Effective Advocacy

Kate Jackson

Warrior for Breast Cancer: Kate joined the ranks of ardent supporters as a result of her personal battle with breast cancer.

Working with groups such as Susan G. Komen and the American Cancer Society, she rose to prominence as an advocate for early detection and research, lending her voice to the quest for a cure and helping many others on their own journeys.

Promoting a broader perspective: An array of reasons Kate is passionate about more than just medicine. She actively promotes numerous causes, creating an impactful tapestry that reaches different parts of the globe:

Animal Welfare: She fights animal abuse and encourages ethical pet ownership, reminding us of our responsibilities to all species. She works with the American Humane Association and PETA.

Education and Youth Development: Kate invests in the future by giving disadvantaged children worldwide access to education and opportunities so they can go on to become tomorrow's changemakers through organisations like Save the Children and UNICEF.

Environmental Stewardship: Kate works with Greenpeace and the Nature Conservancy to promote sustainable practices and increase public awareness of environmental issues because she understands how urgent it is to protect the environment.

Beyond Monetary Assistance: An Advocate for Transformation: Kate's influence surpasses mere contributions. She makes use of her position and power to spur action, increase awareness, and give voice to those who are frequently ignored. She spreads the word about her concerns on social media and at public events, inspiring others to take up the cause.

CHAPTER 11: LEGACY OF A REAL-LIFE HERO

Kate Jackson is regarded as a real-life hero because of her fortitude, empathy, and dedication to changing the world. Her public fight with breast cancer and her advocacy efforts afterward made her a symbol of hope and strength for many with comparable struggles.

In addition to increasing awareness, her openness to share her personal breast cancer journey gave others going through similar problems a sense of courage and empowerment.

She became a powerful voice in the fight against cancer by candidly sharing her experiences and supporting early identification and research. She helped many cancer patients and their families by providing support and encouragement.

Furthermore, Kate Jackson's legacy as a trailblazer in the entertainment industry helped to change the perception of women in television, especially through her portrayal of strong, independent female characters.

Her performances inspired generations of viewers and illustrated the value of diverse and empowering representation on screen by showcasing her brilliance, capability, and tenacity.

Her combined significance as both a pioneer in progressive women's representation and an advocate for health advocacy solidifies her reputation as a real-life hero whose influence extends beyond the entertainment industry, making a lasting impression on both audiences and people confronting hardship.

11.1 Kate Jackson's Persistent Impact

Kate Jackson's diverse contributions to the entertainment business and beyond are indicative of her ongoing influence. These are the main facets of her enduring influence:

Kate Jackson

1. Encouraging Female Representation: Jackson broke stereotypes by playing strong, wise female roles, particularly in "Scarecrow and Mrs. King" and "Charlie's Angels." Her influence paved the path for more varied and influential roles in the industry by altering the way women were portrayed in films.

2. Legacy of Health Advocacy: The public health awareness movement was profoundly impacted by Kate Jackson's advocacy work and public fight against breast cancer. Her willingness to share her story with others encouraged others, building a sense of community and highlighting the value of early identification and preventative healthcare.

3. Trailblazing Profession: As one of the original "Charlie's Angels," Jackson was a major contributor to the show's popularity and rose to fame in popular culture. Her varied career, which included forays into movies and behind-the-scenes work, demonstrated her adaptability and influence on the changing entertainment world.

4. Inspirational Resilience: Kate Jackson is an inspiration due to her fortitude in confronting personal struggles and her ability to handle both successes and setbacks. Her readiness to be open and honest about her experiences speaks to people who are facing hardship and highlights the power of vulnerability.

5. Social Causes Advocacy: Kate Jackson has remained committed to matters outside of entertainment by engaging in advocacy work and charitable endeavors in addition to her personal struggles. Her dedication to philanthropy enhances her reputation as a person who leveraged her position to effect positive change.

The fact that Kate Jackson is still relevant today is evidence of her influence in the entertainment business, her support of health awareness, and her capacity to motivate people via her career and life experiences. She continues to influence opinions and leave a deep mark on the people she has impacted as a trailblazer and advocate.

Kate Jackson

11.2 Recalling Symbolic Events

Highlights from Kate Jackson's career that have had a lasting influence on popular culture and the entertainment business are among the moments that should be remembered as legendary. Several noteworthy incidents and contributions:

1. "Charlie's Angels" (1976–1979): Kate Jackson made a landmark portrayal as Sabrina Duncan in "Charlie's Angels." The show transformed how women were portrayed on television by showing them as strong, competent, and independent, in addition to being a cultural phenomenon.

2. The television series "Scarecrow and Mrs. King" (1983–1987) showcased Kate Jackson's skill at fusing romance, drama, and espionage. In contrast to her "Charlie's Angels" character, her depiction of Amanda King showcased her versatility.

3. Breast Cancer Advocacy: Notable moments that go beyond Kate Jackson's acting career include her candor

in her struggle with breast cancer and her subsequent advocacy activities. Many people dealing with comparable health issues have been encouraged and supported by her bravery in sharing her personal story.

4. Philanthropic Contributions: Kate Jackson's dedication to creating a beneficial influence outside of the entertainment industry is demonstrated by her participation in humanitarian endeavors, especially those relating to health issues. These charitable endeavors add to her timeless legacy.

5. Female Empowerment Influence: One of Kate Jackson's most notable contributions to television has been redefining the story around female characters. Her personas functioned as exemplars, shattering preconceived notions and clearing the path for more assertive representations of women in the media.

11.3 Beyond the Pages:

Kate Jackson's legacy continues to this day, influencing numerous aspects of the entertainment industry and society in addition to the pages of scripts and screenplays:

1. Inspiring Mentorship: If Kate Jackson has coached up-and-coming artists, then one aspect of her legacy will be the impact she leaves on the upcoming cast members and business executives. She helps to shape the entertainment industry's future by serving as a mentor.

2. Evolution of Representation: The influence of Kate Jackson on the development of female representation in popular culture is still felt. Her innovative roles have aided in the continuous transition of women's representations in media to ones that are more varied, nuanced, and powerful.

3. Health and Wellness Advocacy: Kate's legacy lives on through her efforts to raise awareness about health issues, especially breast cancer. Her chats continue to motivate others to put their health and well-being first, stressing the value of early detection.

4. Innovating Women Characters: Kate Jackson left behind a lasting legacy by paving the way for strong, self-reliant female characters. The ongoing struggle for more complex and real representations of women in storytelling is clear evidence of her influence.

5. Philanthropy and Social Impact: Should Kate Jackson continue to be active in charitable pursuits, her continued philanthropic contributions will reinforce her reputation as a person committed to positively influencing social concerns outside of the entertainment industry.

Kate Jackson's impact on the entertainment business and society is so great that it transcends the pages of screenplays and roles, as her legacy continues to grow. Her long legacy demonstrates a dedication to good change and the everlasting power of narrative, whether via campaigning, philanthropy, or mentoring.

CONCLUSION

To sum up, Kate Jackson's path from her legendary part in "Charlie's Angels" to her rise to prominence in real life is evidence of the transforming power of a single person's influence in the entertainment business and beyond.

Her on-screen representation of strong, independent women broke down barriers and ushered in a more inclusive era of storytelling.

Beyond the glitz of Hollywood, Kate's actual struggle with breast cancer demonstrated a different sort of strength, one that was based on resiliency, vulnerability, and advocacy.

It is clear that Kate Jackson's influence goes well beyond the domain of staged settings as we get to the end of this examination of her legacy. Her ongoing effect can be seen in the people she affected through her philanthropy and advocacy activities, as well as in the characters she created.

As an inspiration for future generations, Kate Jackson's journey from glamorous detective to real-life hero facing hardship serves as a constant reminder that the stories we tell, whether on or off screen, have the ability to reshape narratives, defy expectations, and leave a lasting impression on the hearts of those who witness them.

Printed in Great Britain
by Amazon

39812130R00084